Got You!

DISCARD

**Written and Illustrated by
Anna Grossnickle Hines**

CP
Children's Press®
A Division of Grolier Publishing
New York • London • Hong Kong • Sydney
Danbury, Connecticut

To my sister, Nelda
— A.G.H.

Reading Consultants
Linda Cornwell
Coordinator of School Quality and Professional Improvement
(Indiana State Teachers Association)

Katharine A. Kane
Education Consultant
(Retired, San Diego County Office of Education and San Diego State University)

Visit Children's Press® on the Internet at:
http://publishing.grolier.com

Library of Congress Cataloging-in-Publication Data
Hines, Anna Grossnickle.
    Got you! / written and illustrated by Anna Grossnickle Hines.
        p. cm. — (Rookie reader)
    Summary: Sam's older brother Mike keeps fooling him, but Sam thinks of a
way to turn the tables.
    ISBN 0-516-22176-0 (lib. bdg.)   0-516-27294-2 (pbk.)
    [1. Brothers — Fiction.] I. Title. II. Series.
PZ7.H572 Go 2001
[E] — dc21   00-029528

GROLIER
PUBLISHING

"Look out for the tiger!" said Mike.

3

Sam ran away.

"Got you!" said Mike.

"Look out for the bear!" said Mike.

Sam did not run, but he looked.

"Got you!" said Mike.

"You can't fool me," said Sam.

"Got you!" said Mike.

Sam made a plan.
"I will get Mike," he said.

"Look out for the monster!" said Sam.

"You can't fool me," said Mike.

"Got you!" cried Sam.